Fact Finders®

PEOPLE YOU
SHOULD KNOW

ELIZABETH
WARREN

Get to Know the
Persistent Politician

by Dani Gabriel

Consultant: Christina Cliff, PhD
Assistant Professor of Political Science, Security Studies
Franklin Pierce University

CAPSTONE PRESS
a capstone imprint

Fact Finders Books are published by Capstone Press
1710 Roe Crest Drive, North Mankato, Minnesota 56003
www.capstonepub.com

Library of Congress Cataloging-in-Publication Data
Names: Gabriel, Dani, author.
Title: Elizabeth Warren : get to know the persistent politician / by Dani Gabriel.
Description: North Mankato, Minnesota : Capstone Press, 2020. | Series: Fact
    finders. People you should know
Identifiers: LCCN 2019005992| ISBN 9781543571820 (hardcover) | ISBN
    9781543574647 (paperback) | ISBN 9781543571899 (ebook pdf)
Subjects: LCSH: Warren, Elizabeth. | Women legislators—United
    States—Biography—Juvenile literature. | Legislators—United
    States—Biography—Juvenile literature. | United States. Congress.
    Senate—Biography—Juvenile literature. | United States—Politics and
    government--21st century—Juvenile literature.
Classification: LCC E901.1.W37 G33 2020 | DDC 328.73/092 [B]—dc23
LC record available at https://lccn.loc.gov/2019005992

Editorial Credits
Mari Bolte, editor; Kayla Rossow, designer; Tracy Cummins, media researcher;
Tori Abraham, production specialist

Photo Credits
Alamy: Kristoffer Tripplaar, Cover, Phil Wills, 14; AP Photo: J. Scott Applewhite, 4; Getty Images: Darren Durlach/The Boston Globe, 8, David Fenton, 11, John Tlumacki/The Boston Globe, 28, Leif Skoogfors, 17, Mario Tama, 7; iStockphoto: sshepard, 13; Newscom: KEVIN LAMARQUE/REUTERS, 19, MIKE THEILER/UPI, 23, Ron Sachs, 27, SAMANTHA GORESH/REUTERS, 25; Reuters Pictures: Shannon Stapleto, 20

Source Notes:
p. 4, line 6: Jordain Carney. "Senate GOP Votes to Silence Warren After Speech Against Sessions." https://thehill.com/blogs/floor-action/Senate/318422-Senate-votes-to-silence-warren-after-sessions-speech. Accessed October 4, 2018.
p. 6, line 7: Wesley Lowery. "Read the Letter Coretta Scott King Wrote Opposing Sessions's 1986 Federal Nomination." https://www.washingtonpost.com/news/powerpost/wp/2017/01/10/read-the-letter-coretta-scott-king-wrote-opposing-sessionss-1986-federal-nomination/?utm_term=.e8acc5225b7e. Accessed August 14, 2018.
p. 7, line 3: Jordain Carney.
p. 9, sidebar: Elizabeth Warren. https://www.facebook.com/senatorelizabethwarren/posts/when-i-was-in-second-grade-mrs-lee-told-me-that-i-could-be-a-teacher-when-i-grew/971251676370659/. Accessed December 13, 2018.
p. 15, line 16: Elizabeth Warren. *A Fighting Chance.* New York: Metropolitan Books/Henry Holt and Company, 2014.
page 17.
p. 16, line 10: Ibid, p. 20.
p. 17, line 9: Helena Andrews-Dyer. "Elizabeth Warren and Husband Take In the 'Construction Crane' Ballet." https://www.washingtonpost.com/news/reliable-source/wp/2015/07/16/elizabeth-warren-and-husband-take-in-the-construction-crane-ballet/?utm_term=.b094478dd668. Accessed August 20, 2018.
p. 20, line 3: Christ Cillizza. "Can Elizabeth Warren Win?" https://www.washingtonpost.com/blogs/the-fix/post/can-elizabeth-warren-win/2011/09/14/gIQAWdkxRK_blog.html?utm_term=.3d0f794c5b83. Accessed August 4, 2018.
p. 21, line 9: "Elizabeth Warren Comes Out Swinging in Delegate Speech at Massachusetts Democratic Convention." MassLive. 2 June 2012. https://www.masslive.com/politics/index.ssf/2012/06/elizabeth_warren_comes_out_swi_1.html
p. 22, line 12: "Freshman Senator Takes On Financial Industry." https://www.twincities.com/2013/05/18/freshman-senator-takes-on-financial-industry/. Accessed August 20, 2018.
p. 24, line 12: Katie Reilly. "'I'm Here to Fight Back.' Elizabeth Warren Rallied Women Against President Trump." http://time.com/4642418/womens-march-elizabeth-warren/. Accessed August 18, 2018.
p. 26, line 13: Tim Wyatt. "DNA Test Shows Elizabeth Warren Does Have Native American Ancestry in Rebuff to Trump's Insults." https://www.independent.co.uk/news/world/americas/us-politics/elizabeth-warren-trump-dna-test-native-american-heritage-ancestry-a8584561.html. Accessed August 20, 2018.
p. 29, line 3: Martin Pengelly. "Elizabeth Warren Will 'Take Hard Look at Running for President' in 2020." https://www.theguardian.com/us-news/2018/sep/29/elizabeth-warren-presidential-run-2020. Accessed August 21, 2018.

All internet sites appearing in back matter were available and accurate when this book was sent to press.

Printed in the United States of America.
PA70

TABLE OF CONTENTS

1

NEVERTHELESS, SHE PERSISTED

In 2017 Senator Elizabeth Warren took a stand. Senator Jeff Sessions had been nominated by the president to be U.S. attorney general. That is one of the highest positions in the government. Sessions had been accused of racist speech and promoting racist policies. "He made **derogatory** and racist comments that should have no place in our justice system," Elizabeth said.

Elizabeth believed Jeff Sessions would not be a neutral voice as the chief law enforcement officer of the United States.

Sessions's nomination divided the Democratic and Republican parties. People struggled with how to interpret his beliefs with theirs. Elizabeth spoke up for the things that mattered to her—equality and a right to vote for African Americans. Those were two things many people thought Sessions did not support.

DID YOU KNOW?

The president nominates people to be part of his or her **Cabinet**. Then the Senate approves or denies them. One of the Cabinet members is the attorney general. He or she leads the Department of Justice. The Federal Bureau of Investigation is part of that department. The attorney general represents the country in legal issues and gives advice to the president and other government leaders.

Cabinet—a group of people who lead government departments

derogatory—tending to lessen the merit or reputation of something or someone

Elizabeth rose on the Senate floor to read a letter written by **civil rights activist** Coretta Scott King. The letter dated back to Sessions's nomination for a federal judgeship many years earlier. It was about how Sessions had used his power to **suppress** black voters. "I believe his confirmation would have a devastating effect on not only the judicial system in Alabama, but also on the progress we have made toward fulfilling my husband's dream," wrote King.

There is a Senate rule that one senator cannot call the behavior of another senator into question. By speaking out, Elizabeth was criticizing Sessions. His supporters used this rule to try to silence Elizabeth. She was told to stop. She was called to order. But she wouldn't stop. She believed it was important for Americans to hear King's words. Finally, she was banned from the Senate floor. So she went outside the Senate floor and continued reading the letter aloud.

Protesters demonstrated outside Senator Mitch McConnell's house before Sessions's confirmation. They also read Coretta Scott King's letter aloud. King is the widow of activist Martin Luther King Jr.

Later, Senate Majority Leader Mitch McConnell spoke out against Elizabeth. "She was warned. She was given an explanation. Nevertheless, she persisted," he said. Although his words were meant to scold her, they backfired. "Nevertheless, she persisted" became a popular quote repeated over and over to describe strong women—including Elizabeth.

activist—a person who works for social or political change

civil rights—the rights that all people have to freedom and equal treatment under the law

suppress—to keep from public knowledge

2

EARLY ELIZABETH

Elizabeth Herring was born in Oklahoma in 1949. Her parents, Pauline and Donald, had three sons already. Each of them would go on to serve in the military. Her mother stayed home to raise the children. Her father did odd jobs, including as a maintenance worker and a salesman. They owned a small home, but Elizabeth would later describe the family as being on the "ragged edge" of the middle class.

Elizabeth on a visit to the home she lived in until the age of 12.

Like many young girls at the time, Elizabeth thought about weddings and white dresses. She often asked her mother what her own wedding had been like. Finally Pauline explained that she and her father had married in secret. Donald's family disapproved of Pauline. She didn't have a white dress or family at her wedding.

Elizabeth hoped that she would someday wear a white dress. But one of her teachers, Mrs. Lee, inspired her to want to be more than someone's wife. From that day on, Elizabeth wanted to be a teacher too.

DID YOU KNOW?

"When I was done with school, I became a teacher and then a United States senator—in no small part because Mrs. Lee made me feel like I could do anything. Teachers are teaching our future, and they deserve our respect and support."

—Elizabeth Warren

When Elizabeth was 12, her father had a heart attack. He couldn't go back to work right away. Medical bills started piling up. When Donald was finally better, the store refused to give him his regular salary. Instead, they put him on **commission**, which meant he was only paid when he sold something.

The Herrings were struggling. They lost their car. They were about to lose their house. Elizabeth's parents had chosen the house because it was in an area with good schools. Education was something they valued. Pauline decided to get a job. At 50 years old, she took her first job, answering phones and taking orders at Sears. Elizabeth got her first real job shortly after at 13 years old, waiting tables at her aunt's restaurant.

Working Women

After World War II (1939–1945), there was a short period of time when white, middle-class families only needed one adult to work. It was normal for women to stay home with the children. If a woman did work, it was usually in an **entry-level** position that she could quit once she got married. This started to change in the mid–1960s when women began fighting for equality both in and out of the home.

Marchers protested for women's rights during President Richard Nixon's inauguration in 1969. Many others marched to protest the Vietnam War (1955–1975). About half a million people came to protest. It was the first large-scale protest the country had ever seen during an inauguration.

commission—a percentage of a sale made
entry-level—the lowest level of employment

3 › WORKING TO BECOME A TEACHER

Elizabeth worked hard toward her dream of becoming a teacher. She set her sights on college. She took an active role in her high school's debate team. Although she didn't always have the money to travel and participate in activities, she spent hours doing research in the library. Her team won debate after debate. And her work paid off. In 1965, at the age of 16, she was awarded a scholarship to George Washington University in Washington, D.C. She started classes the next year.

After two years of college, Elizabeth and her high school boyfriend, Jim Warren, got married. They moved to Texas when Jim found a job there, which meant she had to leave school. She got a temporary job. But she still wanted to teach.

Elizabeth went back to school. She graduated from the University of Houston with a degree in speech pathology and audiology. Elizabeth and her husband then moved to New Jersey. Elizabeth worked with kids who had difficulties hearing and speaking. Unfortunately, when the school learned she was pregnant, they didn't hire her back for the following year. It was time for another change.

Elizabeth was the first person in her family to graduate from college.

I Want to Work

In the 1950s to 1960s, many employers had a policy that put women on maternity leave after a certain point in their pregnancies. At the same time, the women could not apply for unemployment benefits because they were not laid off but considered to have left their jobs voluntarily. It was common for women to be fired from their jobs once their employer learned they were pregnant. Sometimes they could not be rehired for a year or more after the birth—if at all.

The tower at 15 Washington Street, Newark, New Jersey, housed the Rutgers School of Law from 1979 to 2000.

Elizabeth saw lawyers on TV and thought their jobs were fascinating. She spoke to former high school classmates who practiced law, and they encouraged her to go to law school. She was admitted to both Rutgers Law School in New Jersey and Columbia University in New York City. She chose Rutgers because she could afford it—Columbia cost nearly four times more. Rutgers was also more diverse, with nearly half of Elizabeth's class being women.

Friends took turns watching 2-year-old Amelia so Elizabeth could study. She graduated from Rutgers in 1976. But she was pregnant again, this time with her son, Alex. Nobody would hire her. "Once I had gotten pregnant, my efforts to find a job with a law firm had been politely but firmly turned aside," she wrote. "Everyone smiled, but no one invited me for a second interview. My friends were heading off to real jobs. Not me: I was twenty-six, I would soon have two children, and I was heading home."

In early 1977 one of her professors helped her get a job teaching a **legal writing** class at Rutgers. The next year, Jim's company transferred him again. This time the family moved to Houston, Texas. Elizabeth got a job at the University of Houston's law school.

Life was still challenging. Amelia and Alex were young. And there were very few women teaching at the university. "In that first year of teaching, I was mistaken for a secretary, a student, the wife of a student, a lost undergrad who had wandered into the law school by mistake, and a nurse (blood drive day)," she remembered. And then in 1978 Elizabeth and Jim filed for divorce. She had failed at the one thing she felt she was supposed to accomplish: being a wife and mother.

legal writing—a form of technical writing in the field of law
undergraduate—a student who has not yet received a college degree

Elizabeth taught law at the University of Texas School of Law, the University of Pennsylvania Law School, and at Harvard Law School.

Elizabeth's parents moved to Houston to help with the children. Elizabeth kept her job, which she enjoyed. And then she met Bruce Mann, a fellow law professor. They fell in love, Elizabeth proposed, and they were married in 1980. "Bruce has about a million good qualities, but I want to mention one: Throughout my career, and all the unexpected twists and turns, he has never once discouraged me from taking on a fight," Elizabeth said.

4 ▷ HELPING THE PEOPLE

In 1983 Elizabeth volunteered to teach a class on bankruptcy. While researching, she read about family after family who had lost their homes. Sometimes they didn't fully understand the loans they had signed for. Sometimes the banks misled them. Elizabeth knew the system needed to be fixed. She became an expert on **bankruptcy** laws. She wrote about how financial changes affected Americans. Published in 2003, *Two-Income Trap: Why Middle-Class Mothers And Fathers Are Going Broke*, was coauthored by her daughter, Amelia, who had become a financial consultant.

In December 2007 the United States fell into a **recession**. Senate Majority Leader Harry Reid appointed Elizabeth to serve as the chair of the Congressional Oversight Panel for the Troubled Asset Relief Program (TARP). TARP worked to rescue struggling businesses, among other things.

Elizabeth also worked to create the Consumer Financial Protection Bureau under President Barack Obama. She fought to keep huge corporations from taking advantage of everyday people.

President Obama announced that he'd named Elizabeth the special advisor to the secretary of the Treasury in 2010.

The Great Recession

In the early 2000s banks and private lenders offered **mortgages** to people they knew could probably not afford to pay them back. When people stopped paying their loans, banks **foreclosed** on people's homes. The effect rippled through the economy. People no longer had money to spend on nonessentials. Businesses failed and jobs disappeared. In 2008 and 2009, the U.S. labor market lost nearly 8.5 million jobs.

DID YOU KNOW?

The secretary of the Treasury's job is to support the economy, work toward economic growth, and create jobs for working people.

bankruptcy—a condition in which a person is legally declared unable to pay his or her debts

foreclose—to take possession of a mortgaged property

mortgage—a loan from a bank to buy property

recession—a temporary slowing of economic activity

In 2011 Elizabeth felt that her knowledge would be best used through the federal government. "The middle class has been chipped at, hacked at, squeezed, and hammered for a generation now," she said. "I don't think Washington gets it."

Elizabeth spent hours knocking on doors and talking on the phone to connect with voters.

Elizabeth's work with President Obama gave her recognition with voters and helped her stand out. She also was able to hold successful fundraisers to pay for her campaign, raising more money than any other Senate candidate that year.

Elizabeth knew she could be a different kind of politician than the man who had the job, Republican Senator Scott Brown. "He chose Wall Street over Main Street, millionaires over the middle class, and big oil over big ideas," she said. "We need a senator who will stand up for hard-working people, who won't sell out to Wall Street, who will fight for our future." In the November 2012 election, Warren became the first woman senator from Massachusetts.

Elizabeth's first day as a senator was January 3, 2013. At her first Banking Committee hearing that February, she gained national attention. Her direct questioning of financial regulators showed that she was ready to take on the big banks. She accused them of treating financial executives better than regular people.

She has also proven she is willing to work with others. Although she is known for her very **liberal** views, she has teamed up with her Republican counterparts on a number of issues. "You can tell Senator Warren spends a lot of time preparing for meetings and hearings, which is something I appreciate," former Republican Senator Bob Corker commented in 2013.

DID YOU KNOW?

Elizabeth is an active member of the Senate. Between 2013 and 2018, she only missed casting her vote 12 out of 1,729 times. Most missed votes were early in her term. Since July 2014 she has never missed a vote.

Vice President Joe Biden (right) administers the Senate Oath to Elizabeth in the Old Senate Chamber at the U.S. Capitol. Her husband, Bruce, is in the middle.

Many Tasks

Elizabeth is a member of several Senate committees, including:

- Banking, Housing, and Urban Affairs
- Armed Services
- Health, Education, Labor, and Pensions
- Aging

liberal—someone who favors progress and reform and the protection of civil liberties

5 > WOMEN'S RIGHTS ARE HUMAN RIGHTS

Sixteen days before Elizabeth's famous reading on the Senate floor, people marched. More than 3 million people in 300 cities across the United States showed up for the Women's March on January 21, 2017. They gathered to protest the **inauguration** of President Donald Trump the day before. They also wanted to fight for human rights.

Elizabeth spoke at the march in Boston, Massachusetts. Elizabeth felt the president had a history of bullying women. "We can whimper, we can whine, or we can fight back. Me? I'm here to fight back," she said. "We come to stand shoulder to shoulder to make clear: We are here, we will not be silent, we will not play dead, we will fight for what we believe in."

DID YOU KNOW?

The Women's March on Washington in 2017 was the largest single-day protest in the history of the United States. It is believed that between 5 and 7 million people participated worldwide, on all seven continents. The 2018 march was to show support for women voting and getting women into political office.

Later that year, Elizabeth joined the #MeToo movement. It encouraged people who had been harassed or **assaulted** because of their gender to speak out. Early on in Elizabeth's teaching career, an older male law professor with a lot of power had harassed her. He cornered her in his office, but she escaped. She hoped sharing her story would help other women realize that assault was something that could happen to anyone—and that it was not the victim's fault.

Elizabeth spoke to the 175,000 people who attended the Women's March on Boston Common in 2017.

Unity Principles

The Women's March stands by Unity Principles. The organizers believe that women's rights are human rights. Women should be free to care for and nurture their families in safe and healthy environments. People of all genders, ages, races, cultures, political affiliations, disabilities, and backgrounds should work together toward social progress.

assault—a violent attack on someone

inauguration—formal ceremony to swear a person into political office

PERSONAL HISTORY IN THE SPOTLIGHT

Over the years, Elizabeth Warren has told many stories about her family's Native American roots. Her claim has been backed up by genetics experts. During her Senate run in 2012, her opponent's supporters and staff mocked her with racist chants and gestures. Others have claimed she was given advantages by using her heritage.

In 2016 President Donald Trump called Elizabeth "Pocahontas," a **slur** referring to her claims of Native American ancestry. He continued to use it as a nickname to mock her. "I never expected my family's story to be used as a racist political joke," Elizabeth said. "But I don't take any fight lying down."

slur—insulting name or word

A DNA test in 2018 showed a distant Native American family member. Although this means that her family stories may be true, it doesn't mean that Elizabeth claims to be Native American. She is not an enrolled member of any tribe. Elizabeth acknowledged that and later apologized to the Cherokee Nation.

Elizabeth continues to fight for things she thinks are wrong. In 2018 she spoke outside the United States Supreme Court building. She was protesting Supreme Court nominee Brett Kavanaugh. He had been accused of assaulting multiple women, including Dr. Christine Blasey Ford, who testified against him.

Citizenship versus Ancestry

Many Americans of all ethnicities claim to have some Native American ancestry. This is not the same as tribal membership. Oklahoma, the state Elizabeth is from, is home to many tribes, including the Cherokee. To be eligible for Cherokee Nation citizenship, you must provide documents connecting you to an enrolled direct ancestor who is listed on the Dawes Roll. The Dawes Roll was created in 1893. It forced members of the Cherokee, Choctaw, Creek, Chickasaw, and Seminole tribes to agree to a land distribution plan and ended the reservation system. All members had to be registered.

WOMEN IN POWER

When Elizabeth was first elected to Congress, there were 20 women in the United States Senate. That was a record at the time. In 2018 Elizabeth was re-elected to her Senate seat. The number of women in the Senate grew to 25.

Elizabeth celebrated her re-election on November 7, 2018.

ELIZABETHWARREN.COM

At the beginning of 2019 she announced she would run for president in 2020. She has worked hard to distinguish herself in politics. "Time's up," she said. "Time's up. It's time for women to go to Washington and fix our broken government and that includes a woman at the top." Whether that woman is Elizabeth—or a woman who has Elizabeth's support—remains to be seen.

Women in Government

- As of 2019, 323 women have been elected to Congress.

- The first woman elected to Congress was Jeannette Rankin. She was elected to the House of Representatives in 1916.

- The first woman to hold a Senate seat was Rebecca Latimer Felton in 1922. She served for one day.

- Hattie Wyatt Caraway was the first woman elected to the Senate. She won her husband's seat in a special election after his death in 1932. She served for 14 years.

- Sixty-four women of color have been elected to Congress—38 of them were part of the 2018 Congress. The first was Carol Moseley Braun in 1992.

- In 2019 a record 127 women were sworn into Congress—25 in the Senate and 102 in the House of Representatives.

- In 2018 29-year-old Alexandria Ocasio-Cortez became the youngest woman ever elected to Congress.

GLOSSARY

activist (AK-tuh-vist)—a person who works for social or political change

assault (uh-SAWLT)—a violent attack on someone

bankruptcy (BANK-rupt-see)—a condition in which a person is legally declared unable to pay his or her debts

Cabinet (KA-buh-nit)—a group of people who lead government departments

civil rights (SI-vil RYTS)—the rights that all people have to freedom and equal treatment under the law

commission (kuh-MI-shun)—a percentage of a sale made

Democratic Party (de-muh-KRA-tik PAR-tee)—one of the two major parties in the United States; Democrats are viewed as more progressive, supporting social and economic equality. They also believe the government should use more control with the economy, but less in private affairs.

derogatory (duhr-AH-guh-tor-ee)—tending to lesson the merit or reputation of something or someone

entry-level (EN-tree LEV-uhl)—the lowest level of employment

foreclose (for-KLOHS)—to take possession of a mortgaged property

inauguration (in-AW-gyuh-ray-shuhn)—formal ceremony to swear a person into political office

legal writing (LEE-guhl RY-ting)—a form of technical writing in the field of law

liberal (LIB-ur-uhl)—someone who favors progress and reform and the protection of civil liberties; in politics, liberals are said to be on the left

mortgage (MOR-gij)—a loan from a bank to buy property

recession (ruh-SESS-shuhn)—a temporary slowing of economic activity

Republican Party (ri-PUHB-lik-uhn PAR-tee)—one of the two major parties in the United States. Republicans believe in conservative social policies, low taxes, and that the government should stay out of the economy.

slur (SLUR)—insulting name or word

suppress (suh-PRESS)—to keep from public knowledge

undergraduate (uhn-dur-GRAD-joo-it)—a student who has not yet received a college degree

FURTHER READING

Clinton, Chelsea. *She Persisted: 13 American Women Who Changed the World*. New York: Philomel Books, 2017.

Dillon, Molly. *Yes She Can: 10 Stories of Hope and Change from Young Female Staffers of the Obama White House*. New York: Schwartz & Wade Books, 2019.

Wood, Susan. *Nevertheless, She Persisted: Elizabeth Warren's Fight for Fairness.* New York: Abrams Books for Young Readers, 2018.

INTERNET SITES

About Congress
https://www.visitthecapitol.gov/about-congress

Elizabeth Warren: Official Site
https://elizabethwarren.com

Elizabeth Warren: United States Senator for Massachusetts
https://www.warren.senate.gov/

CRITICAL THINKING QUESTIONS

1. Elizabeth grew up with expectations with the way her life would go. When do you think those expectations changed?

2. Do your family members have a story, or stories, they tell about their ancestors? Do you think those stories could be true? Why or why not?

3. Research some of the things for which Elizabeth stands. Are there things you agree with? Things you disagree with? Explain why you feel that way.

INDEX